INSTRUMENTS OF CHRIST
Reflections on the Peace Prayer of Saint Francis of Assisi

ALBERT HAASE, O.F.M.

ST. ANTHONY MESSENGER PRESS
Cincinnati, Ohio

Nihil Obstat: Rev. David L. Zink
Hilarion Kistner, O.F.M.

Imprimi Potest: Fred Link, O.F.M.
Provincial

Imprimatur: Most Rev. Carl K. Moeddell
Vicar General and Auxiliary Bishop
of the Archdiocese of Cincinnati
June 7, 2004

Cover and book design by Mark Sullivan
Cover photo by Jack Wintz, O.F.M.

ISBN 0-86716-572-3

Published by St. Anthony Messenger Press
www.AmericanCatholic.org
Printed in the U.S.A.

TABLE OF CONTENTS

Acknowledgments

I am deeply grateful to my eldest sister, Bridget Haase, O.S.U., who journeyed with me throughout the entire writing of this book, offered meticulous suggestions for its improvement, and was kind enough to provide the reflection and discussion questions at the end of each chapter. God has blessed and challenged me to have such a loving sister who tries daily to walk in the footprints of the Lord and Divine Master.

I am also deeply grateful to Alf, Mary Ann, Rohan, David and Stephanie D'Souza of Melbourne, Australia. They consistently welcomed me into their Beijing home, and at a moment's notice, never hesitated to seat a hungry friar at their table. Their faithful love and friendship have enriched my life in ways they will never know.

It is my hope that as the Peace Prayer takes on greater and greater significance in light of world events and our individual lives, we might never forget its basic message: as "little Christs" who walk in the footprints of the Lord and Divine Master, we are challenged to look beyond "me" to "thee"—to God and others.

Albert Haase, O.F.M.
October 4, 2003
Feast of Saint Francis of Assisi

INTRODUCTION

The Peace Prayer of Saint Francis of Assisi is prayed in Christian churches and Jewish synagogues. Even my Muslim friend from the Sudan, Mohammed, once told me that he, his wife and two children pray it on occasion.

This prayer has been cross-stitched or written in fine calligraphy, mounted on plaques, framed and memorized. It has been prayed in formal settings such as the United States Senate and the inauguration of Margaret Thatcher as prime minister. It has also been prayed in times of sorrow such as the funerals of Mother Teresa of Calcutta and Diana, Princess of Wales. One of its numerous musical versions has been sung on joyful occasions—at weddings, anniversaries and ordinations. The Peace Prayer is truly a prayer for all times and all peoples.

What is it about this prayer that casts such a magical spell upon us? Why do princess and pauper, bishop and bellhop, saint and sinner turn to it in emotionally charged moments of life?

Instruments of Christ: Reflections on the Peace Prayer of Saint Francis of Assisi is my interpretation of this popular and beloved prayer. A shortened version of these chapters originally appeared in a monthly column in *St. Anthony Messenger* magazine in 1999.

The book consists of twelve chapters, each reflecting upon a phrase of the prayer. Chapter One highlights how the first words of the two sections of the prayer—"Lord...Divine Master"—remind us of our vocation as "little Christs." Chapter Two offers one interpretation of being a peacemaker.

Chapters Three through Eight explore the six seeds that need to be sown if Easter peace is to blossom in this world. Chapters Nine through Eleven highlight the challenges and rewards of looking beyond "me" to "thee." Chapter Twelve offers a brief summary of the book's content.

Each chapter, with the exception of the final one, concludes with four reflection and discussion questions.

I wrote *Instruments of Christ: Reflections on the Peace Prayer of Saint Francis of Assisi* for ordinary Christians like myself, who pray the Peace Prayer but do not always have the time to reflect upon its challenges and implications.

Who Wrote the Peace Prayer?

Most of us know this prayer by its popular title, "The Peace Prayer of Saint Francis." And yet, Saint Francis did not write the prayer and no one quite knows how it became attributed to the saint. The French scholar Christian Renoux has done extensive research into the history of the prayer and aptly calls this "a riddle to be solved."

Though a French prayer similar to the first part of the Peace Prayer can be traced back to the early eleventh century and thus, two hundred years before Francis of Assisi, according to Renoux, the prayer as we know it has its roots in the twentieth century.

In 1901, a French priest, Esther Bouquerel, founded La Ligue de la Sainte-Messe ("The Holy Mass League") and began publishing a small magazine called *La Clochette*. The first appearance of the Peace Prayer was in 1912 when Bouquerel published it in his magazine under the title "Belle priere a faire pendant la messe" ("A Beautiful Prayer to Say During Mass"). Though there was no author's name attached to the prayer, Renoux leaves open the possibility that it might have been Father Bouquerel himself.

According to Renoux's research in the Vatican Archives, the French Marquis Stanislas de La Rochethulon sent this French prayer to Pope Benedict XV in 1915. In January 1916, the Vatican newspaper, *L'Osservatore Romano*, published it. As World War I raged in Europe, that week's editions of the newspaper published certain prayers for peace addressed to the Sacred Heart and encouraged by the Pope.

Around 1920, a French Franciscan priest printed the prayer, now called "Priere pour la paix" ("Prayer for Peace"), on the back of an image of Saint Francis. However, he did not attribute the prayer to the saint. The oldest attribution to the saint appears to be in a French Protestant publication in 1927. During the two world wars, the prayer circulated in Europe and was translated into English.

According to Renoux, the first English translation—but not the most common version of the prayer as we know it—appeared in 1936 in *Living Courageously*, a book by Kirby Page, a Disciple of Christ minister. Page clearly attributes the prayer to Saint Francis.*

Francis Joseph Cardinal Spellman, archbishop of New York from 1939–1967, seems to have had a special devotion to the Peace Prayer. At the celebration of his installation as archbishop on May 23, 1939, he handed out copies of "The Peace Prayer of St. Francis." And when Pope Paul VI visited the United Nations and New York in 1965, Spellman asked for the prayer to be sung during the Papal Mass in Yankee Stadium. After the Mass, Spellman offered a medallion to the Pope with the first sentence of the prayer engraved on it.

Though Saint Francis of Assisi did not write the Peace Prayer, it still encapsulates who Francis was and whom Jesus calls us all to be.

NOTE:

*Renoux, Dr. Christian, *La Prière de la Paix Attribuée à Saint Francois: Une Énigme à Résourdre* (Paris: Editions Franciscaines, 2001).

THE PEACE PRAYER
OF SAINT FRANCIS

Lord, make me an instrument of your peace.

Where there is hatred, let me sow love;

where there is injury, pardon;

where there is doubt, faith;

where there is despair, hope;

where there is darkness, light;

and where there is sadness, joy.

O Divine Master, grant that I may not so much seek

to be consoled as to console;

to be understood as to understand;

to be loved as to love.

For it is in giving that we receive;

it is in pardoning that we are pardoned;

and it is in dying that we are born to eternal life. Amen.

Chapter One

LORD AND DIVINE MASTER

"Lord ... O Divine Master ... "

Linda had taught junior English in the same Catholic high school for ten years. She was an exceptional teacher and a committed Catholic whose lifestyle often challenged the religious sisters who ran the school.

One day she saw a television news report about the suffering of people in Africa. "I heard a voice in my heart saying, 'Go! I have work for you to do there!' It was the most difficult decision in my life. I loved teaching at Sacred Heart. I appreciated the respect of my colleagues and I adored the kids. But years ago, I made the conscious decision to dedicate my life to God. I knew it was a gamble but after talking to my spiritual director and some friends, I felt I had to respond. After all, I had never heard a call in my life as powerful and clear as I did that night in front of the television. I went to Africa not because I wanted to, but because I was called. To be honest, I cried for weeks as I applied to volunteer organizations and handed in my resignation. In hindsight, I am glad I did. It was the happiest time in my life."

I sat rapt in reverent silence as I listened. I couldn't help but think that this woman knows God and more importantly, had surrendered herself as a servant just like the Lord and Divine Master.

THE EGO

The ego is our sense of self-importance, how we feel about our bodies, our accomplishments and ourselves. Additionally, our occupations help to construct the ego. A healthy ego is well aware of its physical image, personal success and effect upon others. A mature person respects such things and does not flaunt them or abuse them. That person is also very much aware that authentic self-worth is based upon the ability to look beyond one's projected image and the willingness to contribute to something bigger than "me." Such selflessness and charity actually nourish a mature person's self-worth.

However, for many of us, the ego is a perpetual two-year-old that screams to be spoon-fed with power, prestige and possessions. And fools that we are, we actually waste too much time chained to the ego's high chair, trying to entertain and satisfy this spoiled child. We cave in to its temper tantrums and selfishly demand position and recognition. We jockey for center stage and the place of honor. By spending so much time and attention on feeding the ego, we become self-absorbed megalomaniacs always primping in front of a mirror and asking the same question over and over again: "What's in it for me?"

In his mid-forties, Eric is a person who is well aware that his shirt needs more starch but is clueless about his teenager's drug problem and oblivious to his wife's depression. A grinder of teeth at night, he has white-knuckled and steamrolled his way through life, which is summarized in his customized automobile plates—"E-R-I-C." He has never noticed people rolling their eyes as he begins gesticulating about his latest achievement in the accounting firm. Tragically, Eric is totally unaware that there is another life outside his own skin.

People like Linda, on the other hand, exist in a completely different universe. They look beyond the horizon of the self and the orbit of the ego. They have discovered that freedom, happiness and fulfillment are found in a life centered on "thee," not "me," and that "thee" is the Lord and Divine Master of the Peace Prayer and those whom the Master sends into their lives.

LITTLE CHRISTS

The two major sections of the Peace Prayer begin by acknowledging a Lord and Divine Master other than me. This direct affront to the ego causes a psychological and spiritual earthquake. Self-serving priorities and self-centered allegiances are knocked off the shelves as a new center of gravity is established. The ground we walk upon shifts—and Linda's experience shows, sometimes literally—as we recognize that our lives are not pieces of personal property upon which we are free to build gaudy monuments to ourselves. In a nutshell, as Paul asks us, "Do you not know…that you are not your own?" (1 Corinthians 6:19).

Indeed, we belong to Jesus Christ the moment we rise from the waters of baptism bearing his name. Christian means "little Christ." As such, our vocation is to model our lives on the Lord's. Paul states the ramifications of this for the ego. In the ancient baptismal hymn cited in Philippians (2:6–11), the apostle reminds us that Jesus refused to be sucked into the black hole of "me" and exploit his equality with God. Rather, Jesus "emptied himself"—a graphic expression suggesting the complete reversal of human nature's tendency and the ego's natural inclination. The hymn uses a striking image and says Jesus voluntarily became a slave. In other words, he freely chose to put his life at the service of his Father and others. In surrendering his will to the Father's plan, Jesus becomes the Lord of the universe, worthy of the adoration of all. The apostle challenges us, "Let the same mind be in you that was in Christ Jesus" (2:5).

FOLLOWING IN THE FOOTPRINTS

Francis of Assisi referred to this attitude as "following in the footprints" of the Divine Master, an image he borrowed from the First Letter of Peter: "For to this you have been called, because Christ also suffered for you, leaving you an example, so that you should follow in his steps" (2:21). To follow in these footprints is to embark upon a journey of words and deeds that chips away at the domination of egotistical pride. Indeed, the footprints of the Master are molded by actions which erase the outline of the ego—forgiveness of the enemy, prayers for those who persecute us, turning the other cheek, compassion for those who suffer and unconditional love. It is a self-emptying lifestyle focused upon "thee," not "me."

Like walking in someone else's footprints left behind in the snow, following in the footprints of the Master does not come naturally. It demands razor-sharp attention and commitment. We may be awkward and clumsy at first, but we know to walk in the Master's footprints requires two conscious decisions which need to be renewed daily.

First, like the Divine Master, we need to mature and break

free from the ego's control, from being preoccupied and consumed with ourselves and our puny worlds. This maturity comes through prayer and reflection, discipline and asceticism.

Praying and reflecting upon the Peace Prayer shine a light into the deep recesses of the soul. The prayer reveals how our pride sometimes hides behind the best of intentions and has wrapped its tentacles around our decisions, feelings and relationships. It challenges us to break free from the mirror of "me" and focus our attention through the window of "thee," thus looking outward and responding to the voices of those who are angry, injured, confused and sad. The prayer also exposes how we defensively seek to be justified and understood, how self-pity insists upon consolation and love.

Over time, as we pray this prayer and consciously walk the journey of selflessness, we break free of the gravitational pull of "me" and are raised to a higher orbit. We begin to ignore the self-serving tantrums of the ego. We begin to see how our reactions to some people are based upon the desire for revenge; how we, like Eric, are so wrapped up in ourselves that we fail to see those hurting around us; how we are sometimes drenched in pride or self-pity.

Realization and refusal of the "me" syndrome are enforced and strengthened through asceticism and discipline. Simple acts of self-denial—from refusing to offer self-righteous words of justification to not buying an ice cream cone and contributing the saved money to the poor—ever so gradually cut the ego off from its life support. We begin to starve it. And as we do, the ego loses its strength and grip on our lives. We become mature as the determination of John the Baptist becomes our own: "He must increase, but I must decrease" (John 3:30).

Self-Surrender

Self-denial is not enough, however. It can become a sickness or disorder if it does not have a larger objective, if it has no greater purpose than the taming of the ego. Following in the footprints of the Lord requires a second conscious decision: like the Master who emptied himself and then paradoxically chose to become a servant, I die to myself and then hand my life over in love and obedience to the will of God.

As a "little Christ," my self-renunciation becomes a gift poured into the hands of God. The self-denial of a disciple must blossom into the self-surrender of a servant. I empty myself of "me" to be filled with a new source of purpose and passion—a "thee"-centered life rooted in God's will. As we shall see in the following chapters, the Peace Prayer shows us practical ways of moving beyond "me" and being rooted in "thee"; it also shows us the practical ways God's will is manifested in our lives. Indeed, this prayer is a servant's plea and a pilgrim's roadmap to becoming an instrument, a servant of God's will.

We begin to pray the two major sections of the Peace Prayer—"Lord...Divine Master"—and the ground beneath our feet immediately begins to move. We realize and acknowledge that the universe was not designed to revolve around me and my petty wants and desires. Indeed, by virtue of my baptism, I am called to walk in the footprints of Jesus who, in emptying himself, surrendering and serving God's will, has become the Lord and Divine Master of the universe.

QUESTIONS FOR REFLECTION

1. What positive qualities do I have? How am I using them to follow in the footprints of the Lord?
2. How am I still feeding my ego? How would serving others nourish me?
3. What acts of self-denial can help me move beyond "me" to "thee"? What new purpose and passion would these acts bring into my life?
4. In what practical ways can I live out my vocation as a "little Christ"? How is Jesus Lord and Divine Master of my life?

Chapter Two

INSTRUMENTS OF PEACE

"Make me an instrument of your peace."

The man was in his forties. For over twenty years, he had been working for a company that manufactured parts for America's military.

"I'm in a dilemma," he said. "I'm finding it hard to justify what I'm doing. I'm not the innocent young employee I was when I started. I don't like making parts that will be used in war."

I told him that his heart was in the right place and that was most important. I also cautioned him to be practical. He had food to put on the table. He had children to raise. He also had to think about his retirement and pension.

He looked relieved. After an hour, we parted.

A month later he sent me a note.

"Thanks for the talk, Father, but I've decided to quit. It's not enough simply to be against war. I have to be willing to work for peace. Regards, Bill."

Bill subsequently resigned his position and accepted a new job with an international bank that helped the economies of underdeveloped countries. His decision taught me what it means to be an instrument of peace.

THE GIFT OF THE RISEN LORD

The first words of the Risen Lord to his disciples are his greeting and his gift—"Peace be with you" (John 20:19). This Easter peace, won at the price of crucifixion, was such a precious gift that Paul began his letters with this distinctive greeting: "Grace to you and peace from God our Father and the Lord Jesus Christ" (Romans 1:7; see also 1 Corinthians 1:3, Galatians 1:3, Philippians 1:2). In a world that was considering Christianity more and more subversive, the disciples were reminded that the death of the Lord and Divine Master—and any faithful servant of his, for that matter—was a portal of peace for others.

The early Christians transformed this gift into a lifestyle. For the first three hundred years of Christianity, followers of Christ refused to participate in battles. They believed the Lord's Easter peace could not be reconciled with bearing arms in war. To follow the Prince of Peace meant fostering the politics of peace.

However, the Lord's gift of peace goes far beyond the "absence of hostilities," as a dictionary would define it, or the destruction of battlefields. As the following six petitions of the Peace Prayer will suggest, the legacy of Easter peace must seep deep down to the very roots of conflict and dissension: hatred, injury, doubt, despair, darkness and sadness—all experiences which suggest a life centered upon "me."

Kay is one of those people who remembers every injury and hurt she has ever experienced. Mention a person's name to her and she can rattle off a litany of past slights and affronts. She has built up so much anger, bitterness and resentment inside herself that even the slightest misstep can cause her to explode with anger. She mopes through each day and is suspicious of virtually everyone. She often sits alone at night drinking heavily and wonders why no one gives her the appropriate respect she thinks she deserves.

The Peace Prayer clearly indicates that if we spend a lot of time in front of the mirror looking at "me," we will never enjoy Easter peace. Like Kay, we will continue to be chained to the ego's high chair. We will develop an angry personality that strikes out at even the most insignificant and picayune oversight. Or we will go through each day seething with bitterness and resentment. Or even worse, we will constantly be throwing a pity party and feeling very much alone and isolated. To put it bluntly, following the example of the Lord and Divine Master, we too must experience a crucifixion of sorts, and we must move beyond ourselves, for Easter peace to blossom within our lives.

PEACEMAKING

To be an instrument of peace means being a peacekeeper who is willing to look beyond "me" and stop the plague of retaliation that creeps into the field of the soul. As Jesus says, "But I say to you, Do not resist an evildoer. But if anyone strikes you on the right cheek, turn the other also" (Matthew 5:39). Following the Divine Master's example on Calvary, we absorb the violence and pain inflicted upon us. We refuse to continue the vicious cycle of violence by striking back, retaliating or seeking revenge. In doing so, we move beyond "me" to "thee" as the internal pain we experience becomes a tributary of external peace for others.

However, being an instrument of peace is not simply a passive, polite affair in which a person bites one's tongue or refuses to speak up "in order to keep the peace." It is not simply a question of ignoring the ego's tendency to want to strike back and seek revenge. As Bill's decision challenged me, intentions and attitudes, important as they are, are not enough when we follow the Lord and Divine Master. I must also become a field hand—an active agent—who intentionally sows the seeds of peace in the world's furrows of distress. I pray to be a peacemaker for others.

Some people in society have no peace. They lack the financial, physical or mental abilities that ensure a life free from anxiety, worry and despair. Due to decisions such as divorce or resignation from the priesthood, they have been pushed aside. Born of a different race, language or sexual orientation, they are treated as second-class citizens with no voice, legitimacy or influence. Indeed, they are the marginalized of society, the alienated of the community and the oppressed of the world.

As a peacemaker for others, I take a prophetic stand by committing myself to uprooting any source of hatred, injury, despair, sadness or darkness that these people endure. I stand up and speak out against any form of prejudice, discrimination or injustice. Though I might speak with the anger of a prophet, I never use violence or incite violence when working for peace. Easter peace is never bequeathed through a clenched fist or proclaimed through the barrel of a pistol.

My goal is not to manhandle my neighbors and force them to change. Rather, my words, actions and lifestyle should compel others to take a second or third look at personal attitudes or societal structures that oppress or exploit the weaker and disenfranchised members of society. This reexamination of attitudes and structures can cause a conversion and the dawning of justice as people move beyond "me" to "thee." Indeed, Easter peace can never fully blossom in a world where there is no justice. Sowing the seeds of peace means first of all tilling the ground for justice.

Perhaps that is why in Matthew's Gospel, the Lord and Divine Master explicitly identifies himself with and speaks for those who have no food, drink, shelter, clothes, freedom or adequate health (Matthew 25:31–46). He emphasizes that every servant of his can be a channel of Easter peace by living lives of charity, compassion and consolation. Through the gift from heaven, Easter peace can continue to touch the world through disciples who keep their eyes, ears and hearts firmly planted on earth and aware of others—of "thee"—who have practical and tangible needs.

Easter peace flowers in Frank who donates his time and money to a soup kitchen in Chicago. I see it in Suzanne, the wife of an ambassador in Beijing, who sells her artwork and then contributes the money earned to an orphanage for children with special needs. Lisa is a channel of peace and consolation in her ongoing written correspondence with a prisoner on death row. A lawyer by profession, Aaron accepts *pro bono* cases on behalf of inner-city apartment tenants and, consequently, is single-handedly changing the living conditions of a section of Seattle.

Such responses speak volumes about the true meaning of

social justice. It is not merely about doing good or being a philanthropist. It goes beyond simply standing up for humanitarian concerns. Rather, social justice is the opportunity for each and every person to live life fully in the here and now. Attained through the lives of Christ and his "little Christs," such an opportunity forms the roots that nourish the gift of Easter peace.

When we pray the Peace Prayer, we imagine ourselves as farmers of the world. Like our Divine Master, we look beyond the pain inflicted upon "me" and refuse to strike back in violence. Indeed, we beat the swords of our hearts into plowshares and the spears of our souls into pruning hooks (see Isaiah 2:4). We then ask for the grace to actively sow the seeds of peace for others. As faithful servants tilling the earth, we wait with great anticipation for the harvest of justice and peace.

QUESTIONS FOR REFLECTION

1. What inner conflicts and dissensions exist within myself? How can I move beyond these conflicts to inner Easter peace?

2. When have I been a peacekeeper and absorbed violence and pain? How did I become a source of peace for others?

3. When have I been a peacemaker and taken a prophetic stand against injustice? How did my action compel others to rethink their attitudes?

4. In what ways can I actively till the ground for justice and sow seeds of peace in my home, neighborhood and workplace?

Chapter Three

SOWING LOVE AMID HATRED

"Where there is hatred, let me sow love;"

According to the *Little Flowers of St. Francis,* the citizens of Gubbio were fighting a ferocious wolf that was killing both animals and people. While visiting the town, Saint Francis heard of the dispute. In a display of saintly diplomacy, the saint brought the warring factions together in the town square and listened to their grievances. He then spoke with them and reconciled them. The story concludes by saying the citizens, years later, were saddened at the death of the wolf. Indeed, they had come to love him.

Though this story reads like a fable, one scholar has suggested that there might be a historical basis to it. What came to be symbolized in the wolf might have originally been a roaming bandit terrorizing Gubbio. Whether fact or fiction, the story portrays a disciple of the Lord and Divine Master who knew that peace is only possible when you sow love amid hatred.

CHRISTIAN LOVE

Having asked to be instruments of Easter peace in the Peace Prayer, we now reflect upon the various seeds that need to be planted if the Risen Christ's harvest of peace is to be reaped within the heart of every person on this earth.

Love is the preeminent sign that one walks in the footprints of Jesus. "By this everyone will know that you are my disciples, if you have love for one another" (John 13:35). However, many of us mistakenly confuse love, both the virtue and the challenge, with infatuation or lust. As wonderful as these two emotions feel, they often originate in the bedroom of the ego and are focused upon "me." These emotions have nothing to do with the challenge of love presented by the Lord and Divine Master.

The situation of the Christian community at Corinth gave the apostle Paul an occasion not only to highlight the importance of Jesus' challenge but also to state the practical ramifications of this love. The community was torn apart with dissension and division. Addressing this situation, Paul reminds the Corinthians that prayers, prophetic powers, faith, charitable acts and even martyrdom are utterly useless and meaningless without love. Surprisingly, he blatantly calls such loveless acts "nothing" (see 1 Corinthians 13:1–3). Clearly, love is the virtue that anoints, differentiates and motivates a "little Christ." Practically speaking, Christian love is patient, kind, and never rude or arrogant. It never demands its own way or seeks revenge (see 1 Corinthians 13:4–7). Indeed, Jesus' challenge of love requires a "little Christ" to break free from the seduction of the ego, forget "me" and focus on "thee." Christian love is emptying and surrendering oneself in the service of another: "We know love by this, that he laid down his life for us—and we ought to lay down our lives for one another" (1 John 3:16). It is not a sentiment or emotion that makes one feel good. It is a decision and resolve that results in the faithful commitment of a servant.

This decision and commitment have motivated the famous and not-so-famous. Mother Teresa of Calcutta spent her life in the service of the poorest of the poor. Martin Luther King, Jr., challenged and helped change the unjust social structure of America. Mev Puleo gave a face to the poor as she photographed their lives, struggles and humanity. With his commitment to nonviolence and justice, Cesar Chavez organized the first successful union of farm workers. The Trappists Christian de Cherge and his companions lived a traditional monastic life in Algeria but were martyred in 1996 because they brought Christians and Muslims together for prayer and conversation. Different people, different lifestyles—but they all share the commitment to love in their own unique way.

In the Peace Prayer, I pray in the tradition of these "little Christs" to plant love in the midst of hatred. This is done by my commitment to help heal relationships and reconcile people who starve from the drought of malice, bad blood, alienation and hatred.

THE NATURE OF HATRED

Why do siblings refuse to talk to one another for years? Why do good friends and lovers suddenly become archenemies? Why do people hate? Though the precise reasons are always tailored to each and every relationship, some similar experiences often draw the battle lines.

I hate because I am chained to my bruised ego, because I have been hurt or taken advantage of by another. I stare in the mirror of "me" and hear myself go through a long inner monologue about what I should have received and never did, why I deserved to be treated better, why I didn't get the respect I deserve, how the other used me for his or her own advantage. I begin building a wall of animosity between the other person and myself. Our relationship is poisoned as I retreat in silence and wage a cold war. Sometimes I climb my wall and openly attack with anger and hostility. In either case, hatred wraps itself around my heart and squeezes until it begins to dislike or loathe.

There is another kind of hatred that I can sometimes see in myself or in others. Somewhat subtle and harder to detect, it grows in the underbrush of doubts, uncertainties or distrust. Because of upbringing or personal experience, our hearts are sometimes cracked with irrational fears of other races, suspicions about a certain class of people, or phobias about being threatened by various minorities or even the majority. Our mistrust of these people, whoever they are, is based solely on the fact that they are different from "me."

This kind of hatred or distrust is usually based upon ignorance, or perhaps said more bluntly, outright stupidity. Within this crack, discrimination based upon sex or sexual preference, ethnic jokes, and prejudicial comments find more than enough room to set down their roots and thrive. Groups of people often become the alienated of a community or the oppressed of society—the "enemy"—precisely because of misunderstanding.

THE CHALLENGE OF LOVE

The Lord and Divine Master states it boldly, clearly and without compromise, "But I say to you, Love your enemies and pray for those who persecute you" (Matthew 5:44). He challenges his servants to become peacemakers who pull up the weeds and dismantle the walls around their hearts—and the hearts of others. This is a direct call to look beyond "me" and focus on "thee."

How can we help ourselves and others move beyond prejudice, resentments and hatred? Jason and Beth's commitment to a summer ministry provides a key to the answer.

Because of inheritance and some wise investments, Jason, Beth and their three children live very comfortable lives in a well-heeled suburb. Cindy is a sophomore in a very prestigious high school. Their two younger sons attend an elite private school.

About five years ago, Jason and Beth were shocked to hear their daughter make some racial comments about the Hispanic workers in McDonald's. What upset Beth the most was that Cindy's words suggested a complete ignorance of the immigrant experience. "She doesn't have a clue about the sacrifices these people made in coming to America," Beth said to Jason.

After a year of prayer, discussion and talking to lawyers, Jason and Beth decided upon a novel undertaking. They have started and are personally financing Bridge Camp. For two weeks every July, Bridge Camp brings together adolescents of different races, religions and social classes in a camp setting. Through recreational activities, shared daily chores, and culminating in the last evening's Culture Night, teenagers from various cultural backgrounds walk across a bridge of understanding. They discover that the wall that separates them is nothing more than ignorance of each other's experience.

Hatred is uprooted, prejudice vanishes into thin air, and people are reconciled when they can stand in each other's shoes or better yet, walk in each other's footprints. This begins with getting enemies together and talking with one another, as the story of Gubbio's wolf suggests. This is the holy purpose of places like Bridge Camp. The hater comes to see that the enemy has a name, a history and a human heart. Acknowledgment of one's presence, awareness of how one's past has shaped a person, and recognition of one's intentions, hopes and dreams help to plow a battlefield and prepare it for the harvest of peace.

Each party needs the opportunity to voice fears, hurts and concerns. We clear the weeds of our hearts by naming, admitting and talking about them. So often our wars are based upon misinformation, misconceptions and misunderstandings. The experience of being heard and understood is the furrow into which the seeds of love can later be sown.

The Peace Prayer reminds us that the first and fundamental condition for Easter peace is love. It is first among the virtues—"and the greatest of these is love" (1 Corinthians 13:13).

Far from being an emotional feeling, it is the conscious decision to move beyond "me" and serve "thee." Love is also the blossom of mutual understanding. As we walk in the footprints of the Lord and Master, we are called to promote the vulnerability of sharing and the sensitivity of listening—the two faces of mutual understanding. In doing so, the walls between enemies come down and the seeds of love germinate in what was once a land of hostility.

QUESTIONS FOR REFLECTION

1. What inner monologues do I engage in that foster animosity with family members, friends and coworkers? Why do I allow the walls of animosity to remain between us?

2. When does racism based on irrational fears and prejudicial judgments dominate my words and actions? How can I overcome this racism?

3. Have I allowed hatred to wrap itself around my heart, chaining me to a bruised ego? What can I do or what do I need to be set free from this hatred?

4. Following in the footprints of the Lord and Divine Master, how can I better witness to the challenge of Christian love and service? What will I do when this commitment grows difficult?

Chapter Four

SOWING PARDON AMID INJURY

"where there is injury, pardon;"

A drunk driver killed Cindy's daughter and mother in an automobile accident. Three months after the funerals Cindy wrote to the woman whose reckless behavior changed her life forever. Instead of venting anger and hatred, Cindy unconditionally forgave the driver of the vehicle—a mother of two children—and reached out to help her overcome her alcoholism.

In her reply, the driver expressed more guilt and remorse than any human heart could bear in a lifetime. "The death of one is more than enough to remind me of my sickness. But the death of two? I don't know how or where to begin to apologize for such a tragedy."

Cindy's reply was surprising and to-the-point. She clearly had made the decision not to keep looking in the mirror and examining her broken heart. "I could spend the rest of my life drowning in pity and bitterness and I do not want to do that. Nor am I arrogant enough to stand in judgment of a sick person. I want to offer you what I know God would offer me if I were in the same situation."

Letters continued back and forth. A relationship between the two women developed. Cindy ultimately paid for the driver's treatment for alcoholism.

Cindy knows only too well that emotional injuries are like physical wounds. The more a person is focused on "me" and picks at a hurt, the more tender it becomes and the longer it takes to heal. It soon becomes a grudge. And that can easily rob one of peace as the grudge becomes infected with bitterness and rancor. Rather than have that happen, Cindy looked beyond "me" to "thee"—to the driver of the vehicle—and consciously resolved to pour the balm of pardon over her. In doing that, Cindy experienced Easter peace as her own wound stopped bleeding.

THE REVOLUTION OF FORGIVENESS

The second seed of Easter peace comes from a teaching that was totally unique to the Lord and Divine Master in his time: "Be merciful, just as your Father is merciful. Do not judge, and you will not be judged; do not condemn, and you will not be condemned. Forgive, and you will be forgiven" (Luke 6:36–37). Or as we pray later in the Peace Prayer, "It is in pardoning that we are pardoned."

When some people read the familiar and controversial passage in Exodus 21:24, "Eye for eye, tooth for tooth, hand for hand, foot for foot," they may find it difficult to understand the meaning of justice in this context. Jesus found difficulty with this passage as well, and consequently challenged this teaching. This caused a revolution in the understanding of forgiveness. He insisted that justice is served not by settling accounts. Rather, the scales of justice are balanced when we freely and generously share with others the very gift God has given to us. As Paul succinctly summarizes the teaching, "[J]ust as the Lord has forgiven you, so you also must forgive" (Colossians 3:13).

Divine forgiveness knows no boundaries, limitations or ceiling. In the same way, the pardon of a "little Christ" knows no reason for refusal. "Not seven times, but, I tell you, seventy-seven times" (Matthew 18:22). This was the saintly pardon that Cindy offered the driver who killed not one, but two of her loved ones. As she wrote, "I want to offer you what I know God would offer me if I were in the same situation." Indeed, to refuse to forgive "thee" is to demand more than God has demanded from "me."

Furthermore, Jesus never demanded that people beg or grovel for pardon. In the midst of his own pain as he hung upon the cross, he looked beyond "me" to "thee" and cried out, "Father, forgive them; for they do not know what they are doing" (Luke 23:34). In the same way, we should never make our forgiveness dependent upon or conditioned by another's apology. It is presumed and unconditional. As we are subtly reminded in the example of the sinful woman in Luke's Gospel (see 7:36–50), some people crave to be pardoned but have never learned the social grace of directly asking for it. We forgive not because it is rational nor because of a person's request. We forgive simply because of the Lord and Divine Master's requirement. It is the fruit of a follower's fidelity and the most difficult footprint in which to step. And we forgive because, as Cindy knows, it is a remedy against bitterness. It provides the cure for closure.

HANGING ON TO THE PAST

Arthur and Stephanie are two years apart. Growing up, as is often the case of siblings born close together, they spent a large portion of their childhood arguing, fighting and competing for the attention of their parents. In adolescence, they spoke cruel words to each other. And now as adults, their relationship is anything but comfortable, loving and natural.

Years ago, Stephanie made the choice not to allow the past to continue to influence her relationship with Arthur. But Arthur, the more sensitive of the two, has not. He refuses to invite Stephanie and her husband over for a meal during the weekends. He ignores her overtures to discuss the childishness of the past. He shuts down when he hears her name mentioned among family and friends.

Now in his forties, Arthur continues to revisit the childhood rivalry that still defines so much of his adulthood. He occasionally reminds his wife of the emotional pain inflicted upon him by his older sister. He doesn't hesitate to mention to his oldest son that "Aunt Stephanie is different from everyone else." Sadly, Arthur seems determined to carry his hurts and anger toward his sister to his grave. He does not realize that his choice of behavior is robbing him of peace and already condemning him to a graveyard existence.

NOT FORGETTING, NOT FUSSING

It takes a lot of psychological energy to keep a wound open, to keep a grudge alive, to drag the past into the present. Such a waste of energy prompts a vicious emotional cycle that can never result in closure. Indeed, the more I choose to focus on "me" and keep a wound open as Arthur does, the more emotionally drained I become as the resentment saps me of my strength and infects my entire life. The longer I keep picking a scab, the more bitterness, anger and self-pity poison my blood.

To pardon is to choose to let go of the past. It is to make the choice for closure.

In order to let go of a past injury, we are often counseled to "forgive and forget." And yet, we often find ourselves unable to forget—and so we mistakenly think we are unable to forgive. But will Cindy ever be able to forget the heartbreak and agony inflicted by the drunk driver? No. Never. Will Arthur ever be able to forget the years of acrimony between him and Stephanie? Probably not. But forgiveness is not about memories disappearing and a wound healing without leaving a scar. Indeed, to this very day, the Risen Christ still possesses the wounds of his crucifixion. But what separates him and Cindy from Arthur is that their wounds are no longer bleeding.

Like the seed of love, pardon is a conscious decision and a deliberate commitment to "thee." In forgiving and pardoning my neighbor, I remember—but I make the conscious decision not to "fuss" over and live in the past. I never really forget what you did to me, but I deliberately choose not to keep picking the scab, not to become entangled in the grudge. I choose to free you from the past by electing not to dwell, mention or remind others of what you did. To use another image, the portal to the past remains in my heart but I make the choice to close the door, lock it, and throw the key away.

Without such a decision, I will forever be staggering among the grave markers of the past. I will continually feel that life is a burden of survival, a journey uphill. Without such a commitment, I will be anxious and restless. I will not know peace. Without the willful and intentional resolve to pour the balm of pardon over "thee," I will find myself being sucked into the black hole of pointless rage and drinking the vinegar of loathing and vindictiveness. That is the evening cocktail of embittered people focused on "me."

In the Peace Prayer, I pray to be an instrument of Easter peace. Having asked to sow the seeds of love amid hatred, I am now reminded that hatred often grows out of an injury inflicted upon me. This prayer suggests that I possess the ability to close the door on past hurts and betrayals. It is a simple act of the will: I refuse to dwell on "me" and my wounds. Indeed, I can experience a dimension of Easter peace by dedicating myself to "thee" and offering love, pardon and forgiveness consistently, freely and unconditionally to anyone who injures me.

QUESTIONS FOR REFLECTION

1. When have I experienced unconditional forgiveness from another? How did this pardon heal my wounds, change bitterness to gratitude, and lead beyond "me" to "thee"?
2. Do I have an ongoing resentment toward a family member, neighbor or coworker? If so, what choices can I make that would lead to dialogue, understanding and closure?
3. Am I entangled in a grudge, choosing to remind another of how I have been hurt? In what ways can Jesus' example of forgiveness help me close this door and enter the portal of Easter pardon and peace?

4. When have I shown mercy, refusing to judge another even in the face of just cause? When has mercy been shown to me, even when I had neither reason nor right to expect it?

Chapter Five

SOWING FAITH AMID DOUBT

"where there is doubt, faith;"

Joseph doesn't recall as a child being affirmed or encouraged to use his gifts and talents. He has no memory of his parents telling him he was loveable.

He does remember being constantly compared to his older brother and reminded that his grades were not as good as Dan's. He has memories of a childhood marked with specific fears—fear of the dark, fear of being left alone, fear of being a laughingstock during his first speech in front of the class.

As he reminisced during this spiritual direction session, I started to understand why Joseph was sometimes abusive toward his coworkers. It became clear why he had become such an overachiever and was controlling and manipulative. Without being aware of it, he was seeking and grabbing from "thee" what he couldn't find in "me." He was looking outside for power, control and success to fill up the emptiness he felt inside himself.

If a child's need for self-confidence and faith is not met, as an adult he will seek to fill this void in ways that are anything but healthy. Prayer, counseling or any kind of trusting relationship can expose such an unmet need—and sometimes even satisfy it.

THE CHALLENGE OF PARENTING

Parents have one of the toughest jobs on earth. Their challenge is to instill faith and confidence in their children. They must treat each child as if he or she were the only child. They have to fight the temptation to compare siblings lest one child feels unaccepted or inadequate. Parents need to encourage with enthusiasm while affirming with affection. In the words of the Peace Prayer, they should sow faith in a field prone to the weeds of self-doubts and fears.

Children who doubt their worthiness, goodness or abilities become stunted adults with no self-esteem. They are restless and "vibrate," flitting here and there for external, egocentric trivialities like power, control or superficial affection on which to lean and support themselves. They are needy and excessively dependent upon strokes and words of affirmation.

The Gospel of John records the Lord and Divine Master meeting such a stunted adult. While passing through Samaria, Jesus encountered a woman at Jacob's well (see John 4:1–42). Since he had no bucket, he asked the woman for a drink. This request immediately turned the conversation to the topic of the thirst that everyone experiences. It is clear that the woman is talking about the topic literally while Jesus is addressing the deeper thirst for wholeness and happiness that is part of the human condition. In order to bring the woman to his deeper level, Jesus asks about the woman's husband. When the woman says she does not have one, Jesus reminds her of her past five husbands and the present one "who is not [her] husband."

The point is obvious: Jesus needed to remind her that love was not about her own "thirsts" or desires, but rather it was about a firm, deliberate commitment.

Stunted adults can sometimes be a burden and challenge—and they can sometimes inflict deep hurts. They might push us away with their humor, sarcasm or bullying techniques. They might smother us with their cries for attention and affirmation. They might use us to prop themselves up socially. Though we might be tempted to flee or verbally attack such people, we are challenged by these words: "Let no evil talk come out of your mouths, but only what is useful for building up, as there is need, so that your words may give grace to those who hear" (Ephesians 4:29).

"Little Christs" need to parent such people by acknowledging their skills, encouraging their talents and affirming their goodness. Indeed, we need to plant faith and confidence amid their doubts. In harvesting such gifts, these adults become centered, peaceful people.

THE CHALLENGE OF THE DARK NIGHT

Doubts can arise not only as we grow into adulthood but also as we grow in relationship to God.

A committed Catholic, Terry decided ten years ago to make an effort at daily prayer. In spite of shuttling her three children back and forth to school and extracurricular activities, cooking dinner for her family, and doing the daily housework, she has managed to find the time to be faithful to her decision. Her daily prayer has been a source of tremendous consolation, a time for heightening her awareness of God's presence in her life, and an excellent preparation for her attendance at the Sunday liturgy.

Recently, however, her prayer has become a real struggle. Terry no longer finds her prayer time giving her the feelings of peace it has given in the past. She sometimes finds herself doubting if there really and truly is a God. These doubts scare her since she would never have allowed herself to think such things in the past. She no longer feels the Sunday Eucharist charging her spiritual batteries. Indeed, it has become a real challenge to remain attentive as her mind wanders to anything other than what is occurring during Mass. Terry confessed to me that she feels discouraged and defeated. She thinks she is losing her faith. After ten years of prayer, she says she has nothing to show for them.

During the spiritual journey, we sooner or later undergo the painful cleansing called the Dark Night. This experience, sometimes—but not always—prompted by the loss of health, our prized possessions or even our loved ones, becomes a spiritual crisis much like what Terry is experiencing. It takes away all that we hold near and dear. Our favorite spiritual practice suddenly becomes uninviting and meaningless. We no longer experience the sacraments as refreshment, encouragement or a challenge.

The Dark Night poses difficulties and obstacles to our faith. We suddenly find ourselves questioning God's love, presence and providence in our lives. We may doubt spiritual beliefs and explanations. Like Terry, we might even have misgivings about God's very existence.

One saint's complaint sums up the feelings of many who experience the purification of the Dark Night: "God, if this is how you treat your friends, no wonder they are so few!"

We need to remind those who experience the Dark Night that it is a natural and normal part of the spiritual journey. People mistakenly believe that the life of faith is like a sports activity or physical exercise—the more you practice, the easier it becomes. This notion was the root of Terry's belief that she had become a spiritual failure after ten years of prayer.

Ironically, the more one travels in the footprints of the Master, the harder it gets. Grace comes into one's life and gradually erases each and every expression of the ego—of "me"—and remolds the person into "thee"—into a "little Christ." Painful as it is, the result is precious. As Paul so aptly exclaimed, "[A]nd it is no longer I who live, but it is Christ who lives in me" (Galatians 2:20).

Consequently, during the Dark Night, my faith is not disappearing; it is maturing. And so, during this process of spiritual maturation and sometimes painful physical cleansing, I am reminded that my attention during whatever spiritual exercise I may practice is to be focused upon "thee"—God—and not "me." Practically speaking, that means whenever I find myself thinking about anything other than God, I must remind myself that I have gotten off the path and I need to gently find my way back. Indeed, every time I hear the ego protest with "me," I am challenged to return to "thee."

Secondly, and most importantly, I need to be patient and persistent in prayer. The Dark Night waters the ground for mature faith where I learn to believe and trust in the living God and not in smug or pietistic beliefs. As a result, though the ego might protest and call the time devoted to prayer "a waste of time," I need to remind myself that the spiritual path to "thee" is paved with persistence.

The Peace Prayer challenges peacemakers to offer the shade of self-confidence and the refreshment of persistent, God-centered faith to those who walk in the desert of doubts occasioned by their upbringing or the Dark Night. In so doing, they fulfill their vocations as "little Christs" who call the world to faith.

QUESTIONS FOR REFLECTION

1. When did I experience feeling unaccepted and inadequate and doubted my self-worth? How did another encourage and affirm me, restoring my confidence and self-esteem?
2. Am I preoccupied by a desire for attention, affirmation and affection? If so, how could I quench this thirst in healthy, mature ways?
3. When have I experienced the Dark Night? How did this Dark Night become the ground for a more mature faith and a deeper belief and trust in the Living God?
4. Am I growing in patient and persevering prayer that leads from "me" to "thee"? How has faithful prayer heightened my awareness of God's presence in my life, making me a more centered, peaceful person?

Chapter Six

SOWING HOPE AMID DESPAIR

"where there is despair, hope;"

When I was thirteen years old, my father committed suicide. It was the first time in my life that I experienced the feelings of hopelessness and desperation. Those feelings were intensified when the family discovered that my father had left behind a trail of debts that needed to be repaid. It would require us to not only sell the house and the automobile, but it would also require my mother, a homemaker for her twenty-five years of marriage and now in her early forties, entering the workforce to support three children still at home. I still remember how my mother consoled me one evening after the funeral. Out of her own shock and despair, she dug deep down into her soul and found these courageous words which she believed with all her heart, "We'll get through this. We'll survive. God will provide."

Jim and Janice stood in stunned silence before a small plot of land where their house once stood. The night before, a tornado had ripped through their small Illinois town and robbed them of their past. They held one another. In each other's arms, the dream of rebuilding was sown.

A victim of mental illness, Bill has been living on the street for years. He looks forward to and has come to depend upon one decent meal a day at a neighborhood soup kitchen. He is grateful that the neighbors who wanted to close down the kitchen decided to keep it open.

What would we do without hope?

EMOTION AND VIRTUE

Hope is an emotion that literally saves us from the present moment we struggle to accept. It gives the near-sighted, fixated on the disappointment or tragedy before "me," a pair of glasses to look beyond—to tomorrow, next month, next year. This farsighted vision lifts them out of their wintry darkness and wings them to a new dawn. No wonder Emily Dickinson described hope as "the thing with feathers / that perches in the soul...."

Hope gives the seriously ill the ability to endure painful operations and dream about playing with the grandchildren again. It gives those unjustly imprisoned the strength to peer beyond the bars and fight for a retrial. Hope provides the bankrupt the energy to start rebuilding their lives anew. It gives refugees and exiles the capacity to endure strange customs and keep alive the vision of their homeland. It offers people living in the midst of war the prospect of returning to normal lives again.

The written Chinese character for crisis, *weiji*, sums up the optimistic nature of this saving emotion. It consists of two Chinese pictograms, one meaning "danger" or "peril," the other meaning "opportunity." For the Chinese, that's what it's all about: every crisis, dangerous or perilous as it may seem, presents another opportunity to achieve life's goal. Rather than being an occasion for discouragement, disillusionment or despair, a crisis opens up new doors never previously thought to have existed, and often brings with it blessings in disguise.

But hope is not simply a saving emotion. It is also a theological virtue. Unlike a natural virtue with which one is born, hope is a grace from God that helps one trust there is life beyond the funeral, the loss of treasured possessions, or the rights and privileges one is denied. It sometimes strikes like lightning in silent moments of prayer and emboldens one to walk through the fiery furnace with a confidence and assurance never before experienced. At other times, it is planted in the cracks of broken dreams and cultivated over a period of time by the words, presence and actions of others.

The Christian virtue of hope moves the attention from "me" to "thee"—to the God who does not abandon creation, who protects, who reaches out to redeem and save. Because of our Lord and Master's resurrection, the "little Christ" knows without any doubt that persecution, suffering—even death—might be the end of the chapter but not the end of the story. There are footprints leading beyond Calvary. God, indeed, is the best-selling author of surprise endings.

Peter aptly describes this as a "living hope": "Blessed be the God and Father of our Lord Jesus Christ! By his great mercy he has given us a new birth into a living hope through the resurrection of Jesus Christ from the dead" (1 Peter 1:3). This living hope transforms every tomb into a womb of new life, every crisis into a potential expression of divine creativity, every peril into another opportunity for the power of God to be revealed.

To the Christian community at Rome, Paul raised up Abraham, the patriarch of our faith, as a model of hope (see Romans 4:18–21). He reminded them, "Hoping against hope, [Abraham] believed that he would become 'the father of many nations,' according to what was said, 'So numerous shall your descendants be.'" The apostle noted that Abraham gave no thought to his elderly age ("for he was about a hundred years old"), nor to his wife Sarah's barrenness. Rather, Abraham simply looked to God for he was "convinced that God was able to do what he had promised." And we all exist now because God was faithful to the promise and did not disappoint Abraham and Sarah.

Our hope is based upon the power, providence and protection of this very God. The Peace Prayer reminds peacemakers to sow the seeds of this God-based hope in those who feel cornered with nowhere to turn, who are precariously holding onto the edge, or who are falling. In giving them hope, those in crisis find an opportunity for Easter peace. But how do we do that?

THE SEEDS OF HOPE

Not a week goes by in the life of any clergy, religious or committed Christian, without hearing the words, "Father, would you pray for me?" or "Mary, please remember my intention in your prayers." How often have each one of us, stuck on "me," looked to an elder, someone whom we consider close to God or who has suffered, and asked that person to intercede on our behalf. And indeed, just by asking, confident that the person will be faithful to our request, we find an interior place of consolation, peace and ultimately hope.

Sister Agnes is a Xaverian sister who spent many years as a missionary in the West African country of Sierra Leone. In 1995, she and six other Xaverian sisters were taken hostage by rebels. The seven were held captive for over three months and had no idea whether or not they would ever be released. As the weeks dragged on, the seven sisters began to lose hope and started thinking that everyone had forgotten them. However, one morning, the sisters heard on the BBC Radio News that Pope John Paul II was encouraging the world to continue praying for the sisters' release. Sister Agnes told me that announcement reinvigorated all seven sisters in their daily trials as hostages.

It goes without saying that the prayer of intercession sows hope. Praying for others helps them feel less alone in their desperation and connected to the larger family of believers. Interceding also helps the despondent feel close to God when they themselves don't have the words, strength or stamina to pray.

We also plant this gift of living hope with our words of encouragement. Even now, more than three decades after my father's death, when I am discouraged and depressed, I still find consolation in my mother's words about God's providence. Those words are a challenge to move beyond "me" to "thee." And indeed, they have proven true all my life for God has provided. Words of confidence and reassurance have a way of becoming evergreens that stand tall and continue to grow despite the frigid cold and deep snow.

Such words of encouragement, however, must be based upon our experience of God as the source of our hope and the rock of our salvation. As the Psalmist prays,

> For God alone my soul waits in silence,
> for my hope is from him.
> He alone is my rock and my salvation,
> my fortress; I shall not be shaken.
> On God rests my deliverance and my honor;
> my mighty rock, my refuge is in God.
> (Psalm 62:5–7)

Indeed, like the early apostles, we too are called to be witnesses to the reality of the resurrection (see Acts 2:32), not only in the life of Jesus but, as "little Christs," in our own lives as well. Without the experience of life backing them up, such words of encouragement seem superficial and will ring hollow.

Sometimes prayers and words are not enough, though. Peacemakers must *become* the hope of others. We must incarnate this emotion and virtue for others. The poor, the alienated and those who have no voice in society, must rely upon us for their dreams to become reality. That soup kitchen Bill depends on stayed open through lobbying efforts. Jim and Janice's dream of rebuilding their home was aided by a low-interest loan from a local bank. Our actions on behalf of justice and peace help the marginalized and disenfranchised take heart for today and have confidence in tomorrow.

Despite the chilling loss of wishes and dreams that surround them, people manage to survive—even thrive—when living hope perches in the soul as a result of the lived witness of others. In the midst of winter, hope assures them that God indeed will send the spring. No wonder Paul reminds the Corinthians that in the end, there are three things that last (see 1 Corinthians 13:13), and one of them is hope.

QUESTIONS FOR REFLECTION

1. When was the last time I experienced disappointment or tragedy? Who or what brought hope and kept me from despair?

2. When have I needed God to reach out and save me? How did the words and actions of others reflect God's providence?

3. How did a crisis become an unexpected opportunity and a blessing in disguise? Did I unexpectedly achieve a life's goal because of it? If so, how?

4. When have my prayers and actions given hope to others? How did this give witness to the reality of resurrection?

Chapter Seven

SOWING LIGHT AMID DARKNESS

"where there is darkness, light;"

For generations the story was passed down that fire had been the gift of the sun god. It was a useful gift to the tribe during the day—and a visible reminder at night of the sun god's care and concern. The tribal members' daily encounters around the fire reminded them of their relationship to one another and to the sun god.

The annual rainy season was now fast approaching. As they did every year at this time, the elders gathered to select a few members of the tribe to be "Keepers of the Flame." These tribesmen would have the sole responsibility of preserving the sun god's gift during the driving afternoon rains. In this way, the fire and what it symbolized would be protected during the cold, dark and damp days of the season.

And thus the gift of fire was preserved for another year and another generation.

GODLY LIGHT

Light is an important symbol within the Judeo-Christian scriptural tradition. It is a metaphor for God's law, God's wisdom, and the word of God (see Psalm 19:9, Wisdom 7:26, Psalm 119:105). Isaiah uses it to describe the Servant of Yahweh (see 42:6) and the charity offered to the oppressed, poor, homeless, naked and afflicted (see 58:6–10). In brief, light is associated with God and a godly life.

Light is a central symbol in John's Gospel. The Prologue describes the Word as the invincible, true light that took flesh among us and revealed "the glory as of the Father's only Son, full of grace and truth" (John 1:14). Jesus, "the light of the world," said those who follow in his footprints would never walk in darkness but would have the "light of life" (8:12).

True to his word, the Lord and Divine Master passed this light on to his followers and set their lives on fire. "You are the light of the world" (Matthew 5:14). As "little Christs," the disciples would be the world's light if they did good deeds, which led to the glory of God (see Matthew 5:16).

The Church, keeper of the flame, continues to preserve and pass down this light from generation to generation. Indeed, in the Rite of Christian Initiation of Adults, the newly baptized are addressed in these words: "You have been enlightened by Christ. Walk always as children of the light and keep the flame of faith alive in your hearts."

THE LIGHT OF FAITH

Theresa is a good example of a contemporary keeper of the flame whose faith has not only been kept alive but has become a beacon for others. Her frail body has been confined to a wheelchair for the past twenty years. At age sixty-five, she is legally blind. She is totally dependent upon medical assistants for her daily necessities.

One would think that such an unfortunate life would have

turned Theresa into a hardened, perhaps even bitter, person. And yet, she radiates a depth of joy and happiness that truly brightens the lives of others. She is the first to tell you that God has blessed her with two most important gifts—her life and her faith—and that she believes it is her mission to make sure that each is an outstanding reflection of the other. Clearly, her darkened world is luminous.

The medical assistants at the home where Theresa resides have often confided their problems, concerns and worries to her. Theresa willingly listens. She also offers wise advice that has been tried and tested in the crucible of her physical suffering and visual handicap.

Faith has given Theresa the ability to see and make sense of the sacred mystery called life. The light of this faith has illumined areas of personal pain and suffering which could have become shrouded in shadows and blurred with questions and confusion. As a result of her disability, Theresa is challenged to "walk by faith, not by sight" (2 Corinthians 5:7). And in a manner beyond all telling, this flame of faith has brightened her path, allowing her to step squarely within the footprints of the Lord and Divine Master, and given her a clear-sighted vision that dispels the obscurity and darkness of her physical handicap.

But faith is not just a private light under which we read the story of our lives. As Francis of Assisi sung in his famous Canticle of Creatures, it can also enlighten all creation and help the believer to witness the extraordinary in the ordinary. It provides the believer the ability to see the face and providence of God in the sun, the moon, the stars, wind, water, the earth—and in those who forgive at the moment of death. Like the sunrise, faith truly provides the light in the daily life of a believer.

DEEDS OF LIGHT

This interior fire of faith cannot simply be centered upon "me." As a "little Christ," I am called to set the world on fire by allowing my faith to radiate towards "thee." The Lord and Divine Master told us to let our light shine before others (see Matthew 5:16) and the ritual of baptism challenges us to fan and keep ablaze the flame of faith. Practically speaking, we enkindle and fan this light in the midst of darkness by the way we live our lives. Indeed, to be a child of light is to do acts that are "good and right and true" (Ephesians 5:9).

While others ignore the beggar on the street and pass him by, Joan pauses, pulls out some loose change, smiles and offers the money in a kind and friendly way. Her act of charity toward a stranger is like a shooting star bringing a momentary streak of light from a different world.

Philip made the conscious decision to move beyond his grudge and forgive the employee who had stolen some $200 from the cash register. And on top of that, he refused to fire the woman since he knew she was struggling to raise two children on a very limited income. Fifteen years later, Philip's son remembered this incident as he himself struggled with the decision of whether or not to fire an employee. It goes without saying that some acts of light have a long afterglow.

Tired though he is after a long forty-hour workweek, Eddie drives one hour every Saturday afternoon to visit his childhood buddy suffering from Alzheimer's disease. Mark lives in a silent, faraway world and is rarely able to communicate with, much less recognize, this stranger beside him. Nevertheless, Eddie is there every weekend. Patients and friends of the home stand in admiration of Eddie's selflessness and fidelity and often silently ponder how they themselves can be such faithful friends to others. Deeds of light often shoot sparks into the lives of others.

Godly deeds such as love, forgiveness, consolation, understanding and charity mentioned in the Peace Prayer, illumine a world often darkened by the ego's hatred, revenge, callousness, apathy and greed. Such deeds flare up from these insights burning and fanned within the hearts of the enlightened.

In a world made gloomy by the false image of a vengeful God, good deeds are floodlights shining upon a new portrait of God. This image glistens with the hallowed hues of the human heart—generosity, love and forgiveness. According to Scripture, our omnipotent God is "the Father of lights" (James 1:17). Such an image is like a bolt of lightning whose crackle reminds peacemakers that a new day has dawned and it is time to put on the armor of light (see Romans 13:11–14).

Reaching out with godly deeds regardless of others' sex, race, religion or mental capacity is also a reminder of the relationship we share among ourselves. Indeed, despite the fact that we are different colors, we belong to the same rainbow. Like the tribesmen of the sun god, we are brothers and sisters to one another, called to share the warmth of the same fire. We are family. "But if we walk in the light as [Jesus] is in the light, then we have fellowship with one another..." (1 John 1:7).

In the Peace Prayer, we pray to sow light amid darkness. Indeed, our vocation is to become a contemporary keeper of the flame. We must fan the flame of faith that has illumined our paths since the day of our baptism. The Peace Prayer reminds us to brighten the lives of others with godly actions that manifest our familial bonds as children of the loving God who, in the words of Francis of Assisi, is reflected in Brother Sun.

QUESTIONS FOR REFLECTION

1. Among my family and friends, who, in spite of suffering and hardship, has become a beacon of light to others? How has this person strengthened my own life of faith and become for me a "little Christ"?
2. How am I a "keeper of the flame" of faith in my family, neighborhood and workplace? What personal resources do I have that help me do this?
3. How does creation enable me to experience the extraordinary in the ordinary? In what ways do I preserve and protect the environment?
4. How would I describe my personal image of God? How do my "godly deeds" reflect this image and my belief in the unity of the human family?

Chapter Eight

SOWING JOY AMID SADNESS

"and where there is sadness, joy."

Lawrence was a very successful self-employed businessman for many years in a Southeast Asian country. He had done so well, in fact, that he, his wife and two sons flew only first class for their annual international vacations. A staunch Catholic, Lawrence believed that his success was a result of his walking in the footprints of the Lord.

Like many people in the 1990s, Lawrence came to mainland China in hopes of increasing his fortune and expanding his influence. However, his hopes were quickly dashed over a twelve-month period when poor judgment led to a poor investment. He lost virtually all his life savings.

If you meet Lawrence today, you would meet a man whose spirit has been crushed. He has become obsessed with finances, especially the money he needs to support his two children studying in British universities. Though he still attends Mass on a weekly basis, he will tell you that God has forgotten him. His dejected spirit often drives him to the sofa where he lies listless, consumed with worries and filled with self-pity and distress.

THE REALITY OF SADNESS

There are so many realities and events which pull us down and make us unhappy: the plight of refugees, the sudden deaths of innocent schoolchildren, the loss of a love, the failed job interview, the struggle with finances or even the defeat in a ball game. From the tragic to the trivial, some episodes raise more questions than answers. Focused upon ourselves and brooding over such incidents, we cannot help but think that God has abandoned us.

Sadness is the ego's knee-jerk reaction to unpleasant situations that remind us we do not always get what we want and we are not masters of our own destinies. Sometimes it is fleeting like a summer shower. Sometimes it endures as long as a season. It preys on different kinds of situations.

Sadness can arise from indifference. When we cannot understand the apathy, insensitivity or lack of interest directed toward others or ourselves, our first reaction is to dwell upon on our own self-righteousness and ask, "Why doesn't anyone care?" That question can precipitate the clouds of sadness rolling into our souls.

We can become sad in hopeless situations. In sickness and death, for example, when we are confronted with our inability to control the outcome of a situation, we often ask in grief and regret, "Why doesn't God help?" Experiences of hopelessness and distress can become seasons of sadness.

Sadness lurks around disappointment. When our expectations are high and our prayers seemingly go unanswered, our instant reaction is "Why?" Disappointments often strip us of our color and our protection, exposing us to a potential winter of despair.

The Babylonian Sickness

In 587 B.C., the Israelites experienced a great national tragedy that pushed them to the brink of despair. Jerusalem was conquered and destroyed, many Israelites were killed and even more were sent into exile in Babylon. For a generation—almost fifty years—they would be disoriented as they lived outside the Promised Land, without the Temple, and seemingly without God's presence. The grief and sorrow of this event continues to be prayed to this very day in Psalm 137:

> By the rivers of Babylon—
>   there we sat down and there we wept
>   when we remembered Zion.
> On the willows there
>   we hung up our harps.
> For there our captors
>   asked us for songs,
> and our tormentors asked for mirth, saying,
>   "Sing us one of the songs of Zion!" (vv. 1–3)

Francis of Assisi rightly calls sadness the "Babylonian sickness." There is truly no better expression. Sadness arises when, fixating upon misery, we feel ill at ease and like strangers, when we are disoriented, when our beliefs no longer support us—when we are not home. We are exiled from the familiar, the known, the expected and the comfortable. In such situations, as Francis suggests, we are prone to one of the deadly sins, *acedia* ("sloth") which causes us, as it does with Lawrence, to give up. It might even seduce us to seek superficial pleasures—sex, alcohol, gambling and other potentially addictive empty enjoyments—as a way to ease the pain, find comfort and grope in the dark for a way home. If it is not addressed, Francis says sadness will gradually produce in the heart "permanent rust."[1]

Rejoice Always

Despite the reality of sadness in our lives, the New Testament letters admonish us to "rejoice in the Lord always" (Philippians 4:4)—even in the midst of suffering and tribulation (see 1 Peter 4:13). But how do we sow joy in the midst of our own or another's sadness and disappointments? In the words of Psalm 137, "How could we sing the Lord's song in a foreign land?" (v. 4) An incident from the life of the Lord and Divine Master provides the direction for finding our way back home.

The Gospel of John records an awkward, intimate moment in the life of Jesus—weeping at the death of his friend Lazarus (11:35)—watched publicly by the crowd. Judging from the crowd's reaction, his grief must have been great, "See how much he loved him!" (v. 36). However, rather than bringing him down to prolonged, self-centered sadness and depression, this event drove Jesus to pray with a confidence unmatched by most of us. "Father, I thank you for having heard me. I knew that you always hear me..." (vv. 41–42). Therein lies the secret to sowing seeds of joy in the midst of sadness.

When confronted with a situation that could have consumed him with sorrow and sadness, Jesus looked beyond himself and focused upon "thee"—upon the God whom he had freely chosen to serve. He approached God with a distinctive prayer. Rather than try and change God's will or force the hand of God, Jesus prayed with the confidence and assurance that every aspiration of the human heart and every prayer are noticed and heard. This confidence became like the wings of an eagle, lifting him above the storm clouds and leading him in the direction towards home.

Like Lawrence, Vincent also came to China to recoup the family savings lost by the collapse of the Argentine economy. After fifteen painful months of trying to negotiate deals, Vincent still had not earned the financial resources to bring his wife and two daughters to China. However, as he told me over dinner one night, "People must think I am crazy. Though I still haven't earned a nickel, nevertheless, I am completely optimistic, upbeat and hopeful. Actually, I am happy! Every night as I go to sleep, I pray Psalm 23, 'The LORD is my shepherd, I shall not want.... Even though I walk through the darkest valley, / I fear no evil; / for you are with me; / your rod and your staff— / they comfort me' [vv. 1, 4]. After praying that psalm slowly and deliberately, I can sleep soundly. It reminds me that when life pushes me into a corner, I have the best possible defense—the will of God! So I need to let go of my desires, surrender and just trust. After all, when all is said and done, the events of the universe and my little life are both in God's hands. It's up to God to decide how they should come together."

Vincent paused and then added, "When we can't trace God's finger in an event, then all we can do is trust God's heart."

Vincent's words convinced me that joy is the sign that the servant is walking in the footprints of the Master while flying above the clouds. Indeed, joy continues to smolder amidst the ashes of sadness when a "little Christ" lifts one up with a prayer of confidence and keeps one firmly on the ground by completely surrendering to God.

CAUSE OF OUR JOY

Christian joy is not simply a superficial feeling of heightened delight or the emotion accompanying extreme pleasure. It does not necessarily depend upon one's immediate circumstances or fortune. As Vincent gives witness, it does not ignore or deny the troubling reality of indifference, hopelessness or disappointment.

Christian joy lies beyond the realm of feelings and emotions. It is a fundamental disposition and stance toward life. It is the knowledge that having prayed and surrendered, God hears the hopes and desires of my heart and will respond in a timely, appropriate way. God is on my side and I must trust God's heart. Joy feeds upon the fact that God stands watch over every situation in my life and comforts me with rod and staff. My joy sometimes bubbles up, sometimes surges up, from the rock-bottom certainty that the finger of God is somehow present in the midst of every tragic and trivial event in my life. Joy is the oasis found in the midst of a confident conviction that the waters of God's loving care and concern never run dry—not even in the desert.

Sowing seeds of joy amid our own or another's sadness requires both prayer—a prayer of assurance and confidence that God is looking out for me—and action, more aptly a servant's surrender and acceptance of consequences. Both prayer and action plant my feet in footprints that lead beyond the tomb of Lazarus.

QUESTIONS FOR REFLECTION

1. When have I felt sadness in disappointment, indifference and hopelessness? Who became a "little Christ" for me, giving me a sense of God's presence and care?

2. When have intense sadness and depression driven me to pray with confidence and surrender? How did prayer, through courage and assurance, lead me home?

3. What does it mean to surrender to the Will of God? How do my acts of trust in God's will lead beyond "me" to "thee"?

4. How do I cultivate joy in my life? How can I, walking in the footprints of the Master, sow seeds of joy in the lives of others?

1. *Francis of Assisi: Early Documents, vol. 2,* edited by Regis J. Armstrong, J. Wayne Hellmann, William J. Short. (New York: New City Press, 2001), 329-330.

Chapter Nine

CONSOLING, UNDERSTANDING AND LOVING

"grant that I may not so much seek
to be consoled as to console;
to be understood as to understand;
to be loved as to love."

Peter felt sorry for himself because he didn't get the promotion. Absorbed in his disappointment and searching for sympathy, he told everyone at work. His colleagues, weary of his complaining, started to avoid him after two weeks.

Susan knew her friends thought she had been impatient and unreasonable at the restaurant. So she telephoned each of them individually to justify her actions and defend what she had said to the waitress. Each thought her phone call was making a mountain out of a molehill.

Allison had gone through three boyfriends in nine months. She was frustrated because she could not find someone to take care of her and give her a comfortable life. She was looking for what someone could do for her—she was, in reality, not looking for love at all.

THE BLACK HOLE OF THE EGO
We Westerners, and Americans in particular, are overly attentive and accommodating to our own desires, wants, needs and

wishes. You need only count the number of times we hear ourselves say, "I, me and mine" to realize we live in self-centered worlds. To put it bluntly, our egos have become bloated and our personal boundaries have expanded so much that we have begun to see the world revolving around ourselves. Indeed, the center of the universe is "me."

Bloated, self-centered egos are like black holes that suck all light, and everything else, into themselves. People literally become "stuck on themselves" as they darken our world. They appear pathetic, defensive and needy like Peter, Susan and Allison. These people streak across the lives of others, obsessed with satisfying their bottomless appetite for being consoled, known, understood and loved. They emotionally drain the people who surround them as they think others were born to cater to their needs and satisfy their appetites.

The parable of the prodigal son and his elder brother (see Luke 15:11–32) presents two people who were both wrapped up in themselves. The self-centered younger son demanded his share of the family property sooner than expected and once he had obtained it, left home and ended up spending all his inheritance. He ended up penniless and in a pigpen—a vivid example of where a self-centered, egotistical lifestyle leads.

His elder brother was just as wrapped up in himself. His self-pity and need to be appreciated kept him away from the family reunion. Adamant about being understood, he was unwilling to try and understand the cause of his father's joy. Needy, self-pitying people have a way of isolating themselves and ruining any party.

These two characters in Jesus' parable vividly portray how people stuck on their own needs end up isolated, lonely and usually frustrated.

How do we break free of the isolation and frustration caused by the gravitational pull of the ego? How do we break out of the constricting limitations of a world focused on me? It requires a change of thinking as radical and revolutionary as that of Copernicus.

CENTER OF GRAVITY CHANGES

The second half of the Peace Prayer gets to the core of what it means to be a "little Christ." It also reveals the true key to peace and happiness as we pray for God's grace to rescue us from the black hole of the ego and shift our center of gravity.

Easter peace is a product of priorities and preferences arranged in consideration of "thee," not "me." Selfless surrender and service to another form the outline of the Lord and Divine Master's footprints. As we pray in the Peace Prayer, "grant that I may not so much seek to be consoled as to console; to be understood as to understand; to be loved as to love." Indeed, Jesus' ministry was characterized by this kind of surrender and service. His healings, table fellowship with sinners and outcasts, and union with the Father's will all witness to a life centered upon and poured out for others. In his own words, "For the Son of Man came not to be served but to serve, and to give his life a ransom for many" (Mark 10:45). The center of his universe is "thee," not "me."

At the time of Jesus, there was nothing more dreaded than the disease of leprosy. The disease was a sentence to a subhuman existence. Not only badly disfiguring a person, leprosy rendered people unfit for life among others and unclean for public worship. It drove people into the desert where they lived alone and apart from the rest of society. Lepers were the "untouchables," for to touch a leper was to render oneself ritually impure and put oneself at risk of contracting the contagious disease.

One day, a leper violates the social and religious norms by approaching Jesus (see Mark 1:40–45). No doubt the sheer desperation of his loneliness, as well as the human need to be touched by another, drove him to the feet of Jesus where he begged to be healed. Most people would have naturally become self-centered and self-conscious if an untouchable approached them so boldly and brazenly as this leper did with Jesus. But Jesus clearly understood the pain of the leper's disease and isolation. Indeed, he was "moved with pity," a Gospel phrase suggesting the deepest pangs of interior compassion. Jesus responded to the leper's request with an action that matched the boldness of the leper's: before healing him, he risked ritual impurity and contraction of the disease by stretching out his hand and touching the leper.

The touch of Jesus was not simply a healing touch. It was also a touch of consolation, understanding and love. Jesus moved beyond himself and what should have been his self-concerns about ritual purity and physical health. He focused his attention on the need of the leper. The touch of Jesus brought the leper back into society and more importantly, into a one-to-one relationship that the leper had previously not known. One could suggest that this was more meaningful—and more surprising—than the actual physical healing.

Time and again, Jesus fostered within his followers this very same attitude of selfless surrender and solicitous service towards others. "But I say to you that listen, Love your enemies, do good to those who hate you, bless those who curse you, pray for those who abuse you" (Luke 6:27–28). "The greatest among you will be your servant" (Matthew 23:11). "Little Christs" walk in the footprints of the Divine Master when they live their lives focused on "thee," not "me." Only then is it possible to meaningfully console, understand and love others.

"THEE," NOT "ME"

I have lost count of the number of times awkward words have tumbled out of my mouth when I was desperately trying to console or sympathize with others. I have self-consciously searched within for wise advice or attempted to concoct a meaningful word for a situation or experience I myself have never before experienced. However, people in pain, like Peter, are not looking for answers from me, nor are they looking for free psychological advice. They are simply looking for a person with whom they can temporarily share their sorrows and upon whom they can lean. They just want a receptive, listening ear and generous, strong shoulders.

To understand another's words or actions requires more than simply noting whether or not what a person says or does makes sense. To truly understand where someone is coming from, I must put myself in the other's shoes. This requires forgetfulness of self as I identify with the other's past and present situation as well as the other's hopes and dreams. Indeed, to understand another, I must stand under the other's experience of life as the Lord and Divine Master did with the leper.

Love is so often confused with an emotion that makes me feel good or an attraction that skews the other into an object for me to possess. This was Allison's problem. In matters of the heart, it is so easy for the ego to reign supreme. However, mature love is selfless, and it is meant to be spent and shared, not amassed and accrued. The love of a "little Christ" is the dedicated commitment to move beyond the ego and place one's life in faithful, selfless service to another.

To receive the grace to be set free from the ego, forget oneself and seek to console, understand and love others is to embark on a journey to another world where God and humans dwell in communion. Indeed, selfless service and sensitivity towards others are like fiery comets shooting across a darkened sky, bringing to egocentric lives evidence of a world beyond their imagining.

QUESTIONS FOR REFLECTION

1. When have I sacrificed my time to console another without seeking anything in return? How did the example and footprints of the Divine Master lead me to this experience?
2. When has someone "stood under" me and taken the time to understand my pain, need or suffering? How did this compassion become a source of healing and peace for me?
3. When was the last time I offered to another the gift of my total attention, sensitive listening and strong shoulders?

How did I feel about the absence of words but the power of presence?

4. When have I overcome my fear and discomfort with the poor and reached out to them? How did this action change my center of gravity and rescue me from the ego's black hole?

Chapter Ten

IN GIVING, WE RECEIVE

"For it is in giving that we receive;"

One day, I was depressed and discouraged. I decided to take a walk through Tiananmen Square. I hoped the fresh air, the kite flyers, and the hundreds of Chinese who stroll through the square everyday would perk me up.

I saw an elderly beggar. His face was weather-beaten and his unkempt hair, wrinkled clothes and dirty appearance were sure signs he had come from the countryside and had spent at least a few days living on the street.

He came up to me with outstretched hands. I hesitated as our eyes locked. In those needy eyes, I saw hundreds of missed opportunities, the pain of the Cultural Revolution, a life in the countryside with no modern conveniences, and the humiliation of begging. With the grace of generosity welling up inside of me, I opened my wallet and pulled out ten yuan (about $1.20), a very generous offering by Chinese standards. He waved it off, pointed to a five yuan note, and said, *"Gou le,"* ("That's enough").

As I handed him the five yuan, my depression lifted. My soul was flooded with light as I received a smile as bright as that day's mid-morning sun.

The Peace Prayer hits the nail on the head: it truly is in giving that we receive.

THE CONTAGION OF CHARITY

This experience is not an isolated event in my life nor is it unique to me. We've all had the experience of watching a sacrifice or gift come back to us a hundredfold in simple ways and in ways beyond all telling.

Parents, teachers, people in the helping professions, and volunteers all know the tremendous satisfaction that comes when gratitude is bigger than the paycheck. Those who follow in the footprints of the Lord and Divine Master and place their lives in service to others are filled in a multitude of various ways. And sometimes their charity can be contagious.

Some contemporary Scripture scholars suggest that may be what happened in the feeding of the five thousand (see John 6:1–14). A little boy's simple and spontaneous act of generosity, blessed by Jesus, shamed those who secretly held and hoarded their food. Seeing the boy's act, they suddenly caught the contagion of his charity and shared with those around them. The twelve baskets of leftovers are a symbol of the abundance of what is received by those who sacrifice and share what they have with others.

Furthermore, the Lord and Divine Master's blessing assures us that no gift—money, forgiveness, a listening ear, a minute of one's valuable time—will go unrecognized. "[A]nd whoever gives even a cup of cold water to one of these little ones in the name of a disciple—truly I tell you, none of these will lose their reward" (Matthew 10:42). It is a promise of the Lord that every time we give, we will, in fact, receive.

THE TREASURES OF THE CHURCH

The story goes that one day a Roman consul called Saint Lawrence the Deacon in for a meeting. He said to Lawrence, "The Empire right now is in dire financial straits. We need money. You followers of Christ have so many valuable treasures in your churches. I have seen your gold cups and silver candlesticks. I order you to give all the precious treasures of the church to me for the benefit of the Empire."

Lawrence surprisingly agreed but said that he would need one week to gather them all up. The consul approved of the requested delay.

A week later, Lawrence came before the consul again. The consul was surprised that Lawrence was not carrying any bags filled with the church's wealth.

"Where are the treasures?" the consul asked angrily.

"Sir," Lawrence replied, "they are so many that I had to leave them outside. But if you would follow me, I will gladly show them to you."

The consul immediately stood up and eagerly followed Lawrence out of the door. As they walked outside, the consul saw hundreds of poor people, widows, orphans, lepers, the blind, the lame and the sick. With great pride and affection, Lawrence made a sweeping motion with his hand and said, "These, sir, are the treasures of our church!"

And treasures they are, indeed! Jesus consecrated them as divine tabernacles in his daily association and close identification with them. "Truly I tell you, just as you did it to one of the least of these who are members of my family, you did it to me" (Matthew 25:40). Perhaps it is a grace and blessing that they will always be among us (see Mark 14:7). Their persistent presence allows "little Christs" the daily opportunity to move beyond "me" to "thee." The footprints of the Lord and Divine Master lead to the periphery of society where the poor, the exiled and the ostracized reside. This is the womb of Christian spirituality and the birthplace of authentic holiness.

"GIVE TO EVERYONE WHO BEGS FROM YOU..."
Father Hugh was appointed by his congregation to be the provincial of the Vincentians in Taiwan. Arriving in Taipei in the early 1990s, he immediately set about getting to know his confreres and studying Chinese. I was amazed at how well he quickly adapted to his new environment.

One day, about four months after he had arrived, I asked him how he was adjusting to life in the Far East.

"Albert, I've really amazed myself this time. Even though I'm in my early sixties, I haven't found this transfer as difficult as I thought it was going to be. Everyone has been so welcoming, accepting and understanding.

"But you know," he continued, "there's just one thing that I really miss in my life right now."

His statement sparked my curiosity as I wondered what it was. Cheerios at breakfast? A bottle of scotch at a reasonable price? "What's that?" I finally asked him.

"The poor!" he replied with a fervor and intensity that I

had not encountered since meeting him. "I miss not having a poor person in my life. At every other assignment, I've always managed to have a poor person in my life to help keep me in touch with the things that really matter in life. But there just doesn't seem to be any poor people around here. So I've decided to ask God to send a poor person into my life. I really need one."

It didn't take God long to answer Hugh's prayers. Within a matter of weeks, a man started hanging around the parish asking for a handout. I often saw Hugh sitting with him, talking to him, and sometimes reaching into his pocket and giving him some money. Before long, the man started calling the parish at all hours of the day and night, asking for Hugh. He always obliged to answer the man's phone call.

After a couple of weeks, it became evident to Hugh that the man had a mild mental disorder. Sometimes he became abusive towards Hugh. Hugh tried to get the man some psychological help and a permanent place to sleep at night, but the man refused.

I still remember the evening Hugh got off the phone with the man, turned to me, and said, "You know, I prayed for a poor person in my life. God answered my prayers. And now, frankly, I just don't know what to do with him!"

"Can't you just tell him, 'Enough is enough,' and say you're not going to help anymore? You might just be wasting your time," I replied.

I could see the disappointment in his eyes. "I guess you just don't get it. I really need poor people in my life. Strange as it sounds, they actually enrich it."

Of course, the treasures of the church are not always as psychologically healthy or honest and sincere as we would like them to be or as the beggar I encountered in Beijing. We've all had the experience of meeting mentally ill street people or being taken by a dishonest panhandler. But that cannot be helped. When society forces people onto the streets to scratch out an existence, they quickly develop their own methods of survival and sometimes learn the art of the con game.

The risk of wasting our time or being taken should not stop us from following the challenge of Jesus. "Give to everyone who begs from you, and do not refuse anyone who wants to borrow from you" (Matthew 5:42). Generous and charitable sharing is a fundamental and practical consequence of the love and selfless service of a "little Christ."

And lest we forget, all our sacrifices and acts of charity form the measuring stick of our own receptivity: "[G]ive, and it will be given to you. A good measure, pressed down, shaken together, running over, will be put into your lap; for the measure you give will be the measure you get back" (Luke 6:38).

The Peace Prayer states the promise of God and the reality in life succinctly: "It is in giving that we receive." And perhaps it offers a further challenge: the compliment of being considered a fool for charity.

QUESTIONS FOR REFLECTION

1. How has a recent sacrifice or gift come back to me a hundredfold? Was my charity contagious? If so, how?
2. How do I actively seek out the poor among us? How does this enable me to more fully live my vocation as a "little Christ"?

3. When am I tempted to look down upon the poor? How can I overcome these judgmental thoughts and feelings?

4. How do the poor, exiled and ostracized enrich my life? How would I feel about being considered a "fool for charity"?

Chapter Eleven

IN DYING WE ARE BORN TO ETERNAL LIFE

"It is in dying that we are born to eternal life."

Martin had been dying for over a year. This was to be my last visit with him.

"How have you been doing?" I asked.

"Frankly, Father," he replied, "extremely well since discovering how to die."

I was intrigued. So I asked, "How does one die?"

"The secret," he said, "is to pray daily for the grace to let go. Over the past fifteen months, I've seen my freedom, independence and privacy fade as I've become bedridden. I fought those losses every day. But in the past three months, I've adopted the penance of letting go and surrendering. They have become a habit for me. So now I'm no longer afraid of death. It will just be another moment of doing what has recently become second nature to me—letting go and surrendering."

Martin taught me that secret to a happy death. And, as I mentioned in his funeral homily two weeks later, he also taught me that letting go and surrendering are the secrets to living as well.

THE FIRST DEATH

Becoming a "little Christ" requires penance and asceticism. The Greek root for "asceticism," *ascesis*, ("to practice") comes from the ancient world of sports and suggests there is a goal to our ascetical and penitential actions. And indeed there is, as Paul reminds the Corinthians: "Athletes exercise self-control in all things; they do it to receive a perishable wreath, but we an imperishable one" (1 Corinthians 9:25).

Our imperishable crown, received after crossing the finish line, is everlasting life and peace with the Risen Christ. Paul tells us that we are mortals on the way to immortality (see 1 Corinthians 15:42–57). But crossing that finish line is no easy feat. It requires two distinct deaths.

The grace of asceticism provides the first. It is "denying oneself" and "losing oneself" according to the challenge of Jesus (see Matthew 16:24–25). Asceticism is the practice of moving beyond "me" to "thee." The three traditional penitential practices of the Church—prayer, fasting and almsgiving—help "little Christs" train themselves to walk in the footprints of the Lord and Divine Master.

Poor Clare nuns, cloistered Carmelites, Trappist monks and the multitude of laypeople committed to prayer, follow the footprints of Jesus into solitary places (see Matthew 14:23, Luke 22:41). That commitment is hard work—in fact, it can be a penance. Prayer challenges us to let go of the ego and its desires and focus upon God and God's will. It trains us to surrender to God's will—to move beyond "me" to "thee." With the Lord and Divine Master, we learn to pray, "Father, if you are willing, remove this cup from me; yet, not my will but yours be done" (Luke 22:42).

Fasting from food challenges us to look beyond the physical demands of our bodies and trains us in self-control and moderation. Jesus reminds us that attention should not be focused upon ourselves when we fast:

> And whenever you fast, do not look dismal, like the hypocrites, for they disfigure their faces so as to show others that they are fasting. Truly I tell you, they have received their reward. But when you fast, put oil on your head and wash your face, so that your fasting may be seen not by others but by your Father who is in secret; and your Father who sees in secret will reward you. (Matthew 6:16–18)

Traditionally, the money saved while fasting is given to the poor and needy. Thus, it too is a call to look beyond "me" to "thee." Furthermore, fasting is not just limited to food, as Josephina reminds me. After working a long, hard day in a restaurant kitchen, she goes home. Instead of watching her favorite television program to relax, she will sometimes "fast" from her program and spend time helping her children with their homework.

Almsgiving is a penitential practice in which "little Christs," following in the footprints of the Lord and Divine Master, "empty themselves" (see Philippians 2:7) for others and share the abundance of God's gifts to them. Like fasting, it should be done in secret and without ostentation (see Matthew 6:1–4). And it is certainly not confined to money.

All of our lives have been enriched because "little Christs" have seen our needs and burdens and emptied themselves in their generous sharing of time, talent, and advice.

These three traditional penitential practices help us to suppress the ego, its will and its desires, the demands of our bodies and the temptation to live in a self-centered world, unaware of the needs of others. Asceticism is the practice of unplugging the ego's life support system. It is the first death that brings us up to the finish line. But the imperishable crown is not yet ours. It takes a second death to finish the race.

THE SECOND DEATH

At many points in our lives we are faced with death—when a loved one dies, when we or a loved one are diagnosed with a terminal disease, or even when we are watching the nightly news reports that detail wars, local tragedies and natural disasters. No matter what the instance, whenever we are faced with death, the clouds of fear come rolling into our lives as we begin to seriously ponder the stark reality of our mortality.

We fear death because we think of it as the end and the termination of our existence. We refer to it as the Grim Reaper who arrives at the final harvest time. The ego looks upon it as the cruel hand that knocks down the house of cards we have meticulously built with our lives. As my good Chinese friend, Xiao Dong, once chided me as he tried to convince me to eat another Szechwan spicy crab, "Enjoy it now while you can. Once you die, you'll end up just like it."

"Little Christs" know, as my dying friend Martin's initial experience attests, that the footprints of the Lord and Divine

Master lead to a garden of agony. All of them must come to grips with the reality of making peace with death. Most do. Sadly, as we sometimes see in intensive care units, some people spend the final moments of their earthly lives fighting against the inevitable and thus losing the opportunity to die in peace. It is the rare person who, due to tragic or sudden death, escapes the mental confrontation—but not the reality.

But, as Martin's dying days also witness, the footprints of the Lord also lead beyond the garden of Gethsemane. "Not my will but yours be done." After confronting the reality of death and overcoming its fear, Jesus looked beyond himself to the will of God. He surrendered to everything—from the kiss of betrayal to the mockery of soldiers as he hung upon the cross. In his final hours, he was still interceding for and ministering to the needs of others: "Father, forgive them; for they do not know what they are doing" (Luke 23:34). "Woman, here is your son.... Here is your mother" (John 19:26–27). Indeed, his dying moments were not the beginning of the end but a continuation of what he had been doing all his life. And that life culminated in his last words: "Father, into your hands I commend my spirit" (Luke 23:46). It was his final act of looking beyond "me," letting go and surrendering to "thee." And in response to a life so well lived, God raised him up.

The Peace Prayer concludes with a stunning reminder that causes the sun to break through the clouds of fear. "For it is in dying that we are born to eternal life." More than a mere summary of the second part of the prayer, the resurrection is the beginning of Christian spirituality, the foundation of our hope, and the imperishable crown waiting for us after we cross the finish line.

"If we have died with him, we will also live with him" (2 Timothy 2:11). As Martin reminded me in his final days, the way we "practice" becoming "little Christs" in this life prepares us for the next. It all depends upon what has become second nature to us.

Francis of Assisi, like the Lord and Divine Master, spent his life practicing the first death of penance in preparation for the second. As he lay dying, he looked beyond himself and exclaimed, "Welcome, Sister Death!" Indeed, he had no fear of that moment. He had sung in his Canticle of the Creatures, "Blessed are those whom death will find in [the Lord's] most holy will, for the second death shall do them no harm." Francis believed he was not dying. He was being born into the eternal peace of the Risen Christ—now a life focused exclusively on "thee"—which he had practiced and prepared for during his entire earthly life. The race was finished. The victor's imperishable crown was his.

QUESTIONS FOR REFLECTION

1. What do I need to let go of in life? How can the penance of surrender and faithful prayer help me do it?
2. How do I personally practice penance and asceticism? How can this personal denial lead to a greater service of others?
3. In what practical ways can I share my time, talent and advice as forms of fasting and almsgiving? How can these practices encourage me to follow in the footprints of the Divine Master?
4. How do I feel about my own death? What experiences have helped me come to grips with its reality?

CONCLUSION

"Amen."

For over one hundred years, people have turned to the Peace Prayer, attributed to Saint Francis of Assisi, for inspiration and guidance. Perhaps we are attracted by its utter simplicity. Perhaps we pray it because consciously or subconsciously, we are only too aware that its words carry the entire weight of the teachings of Jesus.

The two sections of the prayer both begin with powerful words, "Lord...Divine Master." We are instantly made aware that baptism has made each one of us a "little Christ." Consequently, we too are servants who are called to empty ourselves, surrender and serve God, God's will, and whomever God sends into our lives.

The first section of the Peace Prayer is dedicated to peace, the Easter gift of the Risen Christ. We pray to be instruments of this peace. However, Easter peace goes far beyond clenched fists, angry words and the absence of war. Its fullness can only blossom when we have confronted the very roots of conflict and dissension: hatred, injury, doubt, despair, darkness and sadness—all experiences which suggest a life centered upon "me." And so, following in the footprints of the Lord and Divine Master, we pray to sow the six seeds of Easter peace: love, pardon, faith, hope, light and joy.

The second half of the Peace Prayer reminds "little Christs" that the ego needs to be overcome. "Grant that I may not so much seek to be consoled as to console, to be understood as to understand, to be loved as to love." Easter peace is a product of priorities and preferences arranged in consideration of "thee," not "me." Indeed, it is about giving, not receiving; it is about pardoning, not being pardoned.

The Peace Prayer comes full circle and concludes the way it begins, with a reference to the resurrection. "For it is in dying that we are born to eternal life." The resurrection and its Easter peace are the beginning of Christian spirituality as well as the finish line. "Little Christs" live faithful lives and ultimately cross that finish line when, following in the footprints of the Lord and Divine Master, they dedicate themselves to looking beyond "me" to "thee"—to God and all humanity.